The Rope

A New Perspective
On Freedom
and Success

Gary Oates

Stay Right

[signature]

Written by C. Mason Weaver

Edited by Mike Feller

D1488028

The Rope
A New Perspective On Freedom and Success

All rights reserved
Original Manuscript Copyright 2001
by Clarence Mason Weaver

Printed in the United States of America
ISBN: 0-9655218-7-7

First Edition printed August, 2001

Reeder Publishing

The Rope

A New Perspective
On Freedom
and Success

Table of Contents

Introduction

I am often accused of being controversial in my writings about certain subjects. But when these people use the word "controversial" to describe my writings, it usually means I hold an opinion they disagree with. It does not matter if the subject is Christianity, the environment, Affirmative Action, politics, or social issues, I get the same response: I am either invited to "Love it or Leave it," or accused of being insensitive to others.

Some attribute my success to being either lucky or blessed. These people never call me hard working, talented, self-starting, or intelligent. If I defend American values and capitalism, I am accused of being blind to the successes of socialism. Well, they are right about that one; socialism has been a dismal failure everywhere it has been tried.

My opinions about overpowering government regulations, special rights for homosexuals, and a terrible educational system are met with criticism of my motives, but never my intellect. I usually ignore people who try to change my opinions.

However, this is the new "kinder and gentler" Mason Weaver, so I will try to clarify some things.

1. When I say in my writings that people don't need a lot of help, it should be clear that I am speaking about *government* help. If my neighbor gives me help, there are no strings attached. But you are often compelled to accept the government's help. You cannot refuse their "help" when they force you to wear a seat belt or tax your cigarettes to discourage you from smoking.

2. Socialism exists in America, but it should not go unchallenged. I am a capitalist, not a socialist, and I believe the two are totally incompatible. A socialist believes the country runs better when government is in full control. I believe the country runs better when the people are self-governing.

3. I graduated from U.C. Berkeley in 1975, but Affirmative Action was not implemented until 1976. Yet I am amazed at the number of people

who still claim that I received my degree through the benefit of Affirmative Action.

4. Animals do not have rights; people have rights. Rights come with responsibilities, and sometimes rights are protected until one can exercise them, as in the case of an under-aged child. Show me an animal's responsibilities and I will show you its rights.

5. Unborn children *should* have rights.

6. The earth is a ball of mud and water spinning through space; it is not your mother. Trees are like weeds…they tend to grow back.

7. The rich create jobs. I support the rich.

8. Although I hold a degree in Black History and speak Swahili, I am not an African. Please refer to me as an American.

9. Abraham Lincoln did not free the slaves. The Emancipation Proclamation did not free the slaves. Freedom-loving Americans and freedom-demanding slaves fought for and brought about freedom through the grace of God.

10. I do not belong to a sub-multicultural group. I am not an endangered species. I am not a pet of the government. I do not belong to the black race; I belong to the race of Christ.

These are my beliefs and my opinions. Therefore, all of you people who *1)* suggest that everyone should keep an open mind; *2)* preach tolerance; and *3)* constantly stress the need for diverse points of view should really love me. I present a great opportunity for you to practice what you preach. However, if your tolerance and respect for my opinions is determined by how much you agree with them, then your respect is not worth a dime. But there I go again, being insensitive.

Chapter 1

America is at a Crossroads

America is certainly at social, economic, cultural, and political crossroads. Never before in our history have all of these forces combined to the degree they presently have in order to influence the direction this nation will take. Our country withstood the internal social pressures that came about after the Revolutionary War as we were transformed from a British colony into a new nation, and these social pressures were especially severe during the Civil War and Reconstruction. There were tremendous economic pressures during the Great Depression and WWII. In the 1960's we experienced cultural pressures from the civil rights movement and anti-war protestors. And most recently, we survived the political pressures that were the result of 40 years of domination by one political party.

All of these forces have played out on the

American scene, at one time or another, since our inception as a nation. However, never in our history have all of them been so dominant at the same time. These pressures have now combined not only to *change* the American idea, but to *destroy* it.

Even during the civil rights movement, black Americans called themselves "Americans." Today, there are no recognized Americans. Everyone's national identity is hyphenated.

During the Great Depression and WWII we faced strong economic pressures but never considered ourselves helpless or hopeless. There was very little panic among the people. We just came together as a nation and worked our way through it. We assumed that hard work would prevail—and it did. But today, every problem becomes a major crisis and we are paralyzed until some form of government action is taken to solve it.

In the 2000 presidential election the Democratic candidate promised a bigger federal government that would have more central control over our lives. Yet one-half of

America voted for him!

That election should have been a wake-up call for America. We had two completely different candidates to choose from. It was a very clear choice on every issue. It was a test of our education, self worth, self-determination, and national identity. It was a test of how we looked at each other and ourselves. *Were we slaves who were content pleasing master, or prisoners looking to escape the prison?*

We went to the polls in November of 2000 and looked our choices right in the eye. After decades of teaching our children nothing about American principles—not to mention *ideals*—we had to choose between principles and deceit. The choices were clear: We had promises of better treatment on the plantation of fear, crisis, and hopelessness...or the promise of freedom and independence.

The trials and choices were not the reason we were at a crossroads; the results were the telling points. With so many obvious proofs and clear national indications, half the nation's voters still voted to please master and did not vote for freedom.

This is a common phenomenon within a slave society and with individuals who have a slave mentality. The slaves would always support master. They thought their only hope was to get the best job on the plantation, but never to actually get *free* from the plantation. Sure, master treated them rough; but he was master and he fed them.

Master was responsible to provide their jobs, their homes, their medication, their retirement, their safety, and their children with an education. The slaves never considered any of these to be *their* responsibility. The slaves thought they had a "right" to these from master because they had toiled so long in master's fields.

The mentality of a slave is to not be free, but to be *better managed* by master. Given the chance, he will usually choose a "better" master rather than freedom. Master understands this and uses it constantly to keep his slaves in check. All thoughts of independence are discouraged. He cannot allow thoughts of freedom to interfere with the slave mentality.

The fact that half the nation voted for more government control over their lives proves that we are now in a plantation mentality. The choices were simple. One party promised more and better management of your life; the other promised to get out of your life and let you manage it yourself.

Half the nation thought it was strange and dangerous to be free. "Who will give me my prescription medicine?" They could not fathom getting their needed daily services from any source other than the government. These people voted for the best master because they cannot understand the concept of freedom.

But master understands slavery and what motivates a slave's dedication to his master. THE ECONOMY! Whoever controls the bread controls the actions. There is something wrong with a system that will allow you to work and pay taxes for 30 years and then let you end up taking tickets at a movie theater *after* you retire.

Master ensures that you retire broke and will continue to depend upon his kindness for your medications and other expenses. If you vote for him, he will take care of you and your children.

15

Economic freedom is real freedom! Master knows this and in this book I will explain his plan to you.

The slave mentality

What is the "slave mentality"? It is the same internal force that keeps an abused woman with her man. She will defend him to others, fight the police who come to her rescue, and then return to him—giving him more love the more he abuses her.

She thinks of herself as useless without him and unable to take care of herself or her children. She believes that if she loves him just a little more, he will stop beating her. If she has more babies for him, he will no longer cheat on her.

Her friends and relatives cannot tell her to leave him; she doesn't understand. If they take her away, she will return to him. If he leaves her, she will find someone just like him to abuse her more. You cannot tell her to leave because she believes there is no life away from him.

The abuser has convinced her that she is useless, unattractive, and incapable of making it on her own. She has such low self-esteem that she will reject anyone who tries to help her. She feels better denying herself freedom because she doesn't think she *deserves* to be happy.

She will go to work and lie about her black eye. She will wear a smile while crying underneath. An abused wife thinks her life and lifestyle depend upon how well she pleases her master. Even with the door of escape wide open, many abused women will not leave.

The plantation mentality functions in much the same way as a small child. Everything a child needs requires some action on a parent's part first. If the child is hungry, a parent must act. When the child is sick, a parent must act. To get the child to bed or get up, dressed, and washed to go out requires a parent's permission and action.

A child knows he cannot do anything without input from a parent. The child would not even understand the concept of independence from the parent. A young child would be afraid of you if you suggested that they could be free from the dominance of that parent. They would ask, *"Who will feed me?"* They would think you hated them because you were trying to get them to function independently of the parent.

The plantation mentality is the belief that your economic livelihood is the concern and responsibility of others who, in truth, don't care about you at all. In this mental state, saving your own money for retirement becomes "risky," but allowing others to ensure a limited retirement lifestyle for you is much more secure. Working hard for the benefit of others becomes the norm and working for yourself and your family becomes "selfish."

You will find that the very notion of owning your own business is alien to your friends and relatives. You will experience resentment and even hostility from others. There's a reason for such hostility: you are thinking like a prisoner and they are thinking like a slave.

Question: Are we going to be slaves to the government or masters of our own independence?

To an independent-thinking person the notion of freedom will never be confused with one of safety. We must decide both as a nation and as independent people if we want the government to keep us safe or allow us to be free.

In order for the government to keep us safe, they must control us. It must force mandates and regulations on businesses to ensure a certain "quality of life" for workers. It must control our driving and make sure we put on seat belts for our own protection. The government must tell business owners whom to hire based upon its own criteria, when employees can take vacations and leaves of absences, and how and when they can be fired. In order to keep you safe the government will also tell you how to educate your children and even what type of careers they will have. For our safety and security, the government has taken over most of our retirement plans, our medical insurance, and our daily lives. When we are afraid and ask for help, the government's response is to take more power and freedoms from us.

For us to remain free, we, the people, must control the government. We have vested power in the government to protect certain rights for us. One is to ensure domestic tranquility, and another is the pursuit of happiness. However, the Founding Fathers never envisioned the "nanny-state" government we now have. Independent, free people no longer have any freedom *from* the government. Everything we do is, to some degree, controlled by the government. But the Founders designed our system of government in such a way that we were supposed to be a self-governing people.

Responsibility comes with freedom. It is what you are fully responsible for, not whom you must fully rely upon. Show me someone who is responsible and I will show you someone who is free.

If your income is too low and you would rather get a small raise from master instead of owning your own business, you have a slave mentality. If your refrigerator is empty and you seek more government cheese, you are a slave. If you think every problem requires a government solution, you are not thinking independently. If you depend upon others for your safety, security, and economic well-being, you will continue to look for the best master to serve and he will always have a plan for you. *What is your plan for yourself?*

Chapter 2

We Need To Take Back Our Independence

Independence means freedom. It also requires responsibility. This means that in order for you to be free, every problem you face must be *your* responsibility to solve and no one else's. If you want a better home, more income, less stress, or a better lifestyle, it requires some action on *your* part and no one else's.

Today, we are constantly reminded that the economic concept of financial independence is negative, foreign, and impossible to achieve. Like the slaves in America's past, these people consider freedom to be dangerous. Therefore, they have taught us to believe that real freedom is secured through government programs—even when the evidence clearly shows the opposite to be true. Most of us cannot name a government program that has worked—especially a social program.

You are told that learning to depend on yourself will harm not only you but the entire slave camp as well. Master cannot lower your taxes because the slave camp will be harmed. Master cannot give you control over your schools because you might not teach your children to serve master's children. And, of course, there can be no real retirement savings program: you may be able to free your children from the economic dependency master relies upon.

FREEDOM IS NEVER FREE! It requires the diligent, sacrificial watch of faithful men and women. It must be guarded and nurtured. Freedom does not protect you; you must protect it. If you are not willing to sacrifice for freedom, you will not have it for very long.

Guess what? If you really want to be free, you must understand some things.

1. Master is the problem; therefore, he cannot be the solution.
2. Master is an expert on slavery, not

freedom. Do not get your information from him.
3. Master's plan will only benefit master. Have your own Master Plan.
4. Master can only control through fear. Fear is a lack of courage in your own solution. Don't turn to master for *his* solution.

The real heroes—independent business owners

During the days of the Underground Railroad, master was afraid of freedom fighters—those people who were trying to take the slaves away from master's control. The freedom fighters included both the abolitionists who supported the movement and the escaped slaves themselves who returned to their plantations to break the chains of bondage and lead others to freedom. Even today, the slaves have been trained to distrust the freedom fighters that are the very agents of freedom that can help them win their *own* freedom. Do not forget, the slaves have been taught through generations of social indoctrination to love master and hate the freedom fighters. So when your friend thinks about starting his own business, he is often greeted with skepticism—even from his close friends and relatives. The entrepreneur sprit is the true American spirit. It was the entrepreneur spirit that forged the way westward and created small business opportunities for so many people.

Independent business owners have always been a threat to master and his plantation mentality. If you are struggling to build your own business, you are also struggling to develop an independent mentality. Master cannot remain master if the slaves are constantly trying to become free.

He will try to discourage your business development as much as he can. He will tax your profits, add restrictions onto your work, and he will license your very existence—all to limit or corrupt your profits.

As a business owner you will find that master controls every movement of your money. You are taxed or assessed a fee every time you move your money; and the payroll tax, employee tax, business license, import fees, city license, workmen's compensation, unemployment tax, FICA, state disability tax,

Social Security tax, and much more are all designed to tangle you up into a dependency on master. Like it or not, the government becomes a non-working, non-contributing partner in every business. Name a business you can legitimately go into without first obtaining a business license—which, in reality, is nothing more than getting permission from master.

Until recently, most jobs were created by small businesses. But today, most jobs are created by the government. The willingness to sacrifice everything one has for a business creates a deep loyalty to the surrounding community. It links the community, which, in turn, contributes to the success of the small business. This is the avenue to success for your business. This is why there continues to be such an intense and sustained attack on real families and real communities.

Liberal, extremist organizations are using political elites in the media and academia to change the traditional definition of families, communities, and Americans. We now have "alternative families" and "communities" that are based on race, sexual preference, or nationality—anything, of course, except the American nationality.

During the years of institutionalized slavery we had "slave communities," not a community of slaves. A normal community is based upon a mother and father raising their children together with other families similar to their own. Wives could depend upon other women to help keep the community's standards, and husbands could depend upon other men to defend and protect the family.

A slave community was just the opposite. Husbands and wives were not important. They were not defined by the neighborhood or their principles. They were defined by master's subdivisions. You had field slaves and house slaves. There were "big plantation" slaves and those from smaller ones. There was the harvest group as well as the shipping-to-market group. What we *did not* have were men depending upon other men, women depending upon other women, and *everyone* depending upon each other. All slave group subdivisions had one thing in common, though: they all were dependent upon master.

A normal, healthy system would bring confusion to master's system. Therefore, master could not allow individual male slaves to have dominance over their wives and the babies they made.

It is the same today. Our communities have been redefined into that of the old slave system. We no longer have community identity. We are identified by our master's designation. We have the black community, the homosexual community, the Christian community...or whatever else master decides. But we will never have a community of families seeking to maintain their own quest for domestic tranquility and the pursuit of happiness as long as the government continues to implement anti-family policies and programs.

Both have been removed and substituted by dependency and the pursuit of safety. If we have individual goals, we are called selfish. If we have deeply-held religious beliefs, we are called intolerant. If we think our children can be the best, we are called mean-spirited. If we dare try to own a business, we are called hateful and greedy.

The real heroes of America are the hardworking men and women who are struggling to provide for their families and pass on a legacy to their children. These men and women are looking for a way to provide a better existence for their children. They are determined to find a better way, and will not allow the negative, God-hating mannerisms of master stop them.

Those who are building companies despite harsh government regulations and controls are America's real heroes. They possess the Spirit of 1776—the can-do spirit of America's past. The spirit that did the impossible with the improbable. A people that survived WWI and the Great Depression. A spirit that raised children who defeated our enemies in WWII. This was the spirit of the past generation whose children went to the moon and tore down the Berlin Wall.

Nothing was impossible to them. If a mountain were in their way, they would move the mountain. If no roads existed to their destination, they would not change destinations; they would build those roads.

They were free, not perfect. They had problems getting along with each other. They had a lot of inner healing to do as a nation; but if you threatened the freedom and independence of any, you had to deal with the whole.

They were not slaves. Some were prisoners, but all were willing to sacrifice for freedom. To sacrifice for freedom means that you are also willing to sacrifice for someone *else's* freedom.

Chapter 3

Slaves vs. Prisoners

The reason your friends don't get it is because they are slaves and you are a prisoner looking for a way to escape

SLAVES

There are two distinct categories of people under master's domination on the plantation. Some are *slaves* and some are *prisoners*. They look alike on the surface, but are motivated by completely different mental forces. Which one are you? How can you tell the difference? If you are building a business, you only want fellow prisoners around you—never slaves.

A slave is a person who has accepted the power master has over his life. He has not only accepted it, he believes it is natural. He does not understand real freedom because he thinks that any freedom he *does* have is connected to the way master provides for him.

Therefore, the slave will serve master with a patriotic fervor. He will brag about the great job he has managing master's plantation for him. He will wear the company logo, attend all of the union meetings, and wait patiently for his 30-year retirement dinner. He believes loyalty to master will ensure his exalted position even after retirement.

But every problem he has requires master's attention and action. If he needs supervision for his children, master must place a daycare center at the job. If he does not have enough money for food, master must give him more government food. If he gets sick, master should provide a better medical program for his slaves.

This slave also feels threatened by any independent-thinking person. He will resist any talk about self-reliance and will be very disappointed in your announcement of freedom from master. Not only will he be unable to understand your decision, he will fight against your efforts to succeed. He will be determined to see that you—and all who are with you—should fail.

PRISONERS

While a slave will spend all of his life trying to please master and pretend he is free, a prisoner will spend his entire life trying to escape dependency upon master.

If someone is locked up in prison, they do not have to be told they are prisoners. They know that freedom is right over the wall. They look at the wall all day and only think about ways to get over it. While they are prisoners they will eat the prison food and dress in prison clothes, but their minds are not on pleasing the guards or the warden. A prisoner will spend all of his life trying to dig a hole through a concrete wall using a spoon.

He will never give up on freedom and his children will be trained to seek freedom also. (That is why master must also control the prisoner's children.) He will look at others who have escaped and imitate them, trying almost anything in his quest for freedom. Freedom is his motivation, not appeasement.

This is the kind of person who will start 10 businesses, fail 10 times, and ignore your laughter as he tries number 11. He understands real freedom when he sees it. He will not be fooled by "near freedom" or some kind of agreement with the prison guards to go easy on him. This person knows that real freedom means economic freedom—and he will not settle for anything less. He also knows that there is no economic freedom unless you control the venue to economic freedom. You must find a way to create wealth that *you* control. It must be a formula and mental state of being that no one can take from you. This is what a prisoner is looking for.

It has been said that liberals are for the poor and conservatives are for the rich—which did I want to be?

In the 1960's I remember my college professors saying that liberals were for the poor and conservatives were for the rich. They intended for me to think that being a liberal was good and being a conservative was bad. *Who could be against the poor? Who could hate the poor?* I considered myself a liberal because I considered myself to be a nice person.

However, I began to notice something. Liberals were very good at *managing* the poor, but not at getting them out of poverty. As I worked for liberal politicians and organizations I finally understood what they were really saying.

Liberals are for *poverty*, not the poor! They understand poverty and want to make you very comfortable in your poverty. Liberals want you to accept not only your poverty, but also your dependency upon them to feed and care for you. Liberals do not want to allow you any freedom of thought, nor do they want you to desire independence from them. They are your poverty managers and anything you need must come from them as your overseers.

Liberals understood the dynamics of poverty and dependency a long time ago and figured out how to grow them both. It occurred to me after reading and thinking about the *sources* of poverty and dependency. Here is the secret that I discovered as a young Berkeley student. It helped me to understand how we could spend so much money on poverty and still have so much more poverty.

I discovered that liberals were very good at keeping people poor, both in spirit and in thought. Liberals understood one thing. They knew that if you placed poor people in *one* neighborhood something magical would happen. I do not care if it was an Indian reservation, a trailer park, or an inner-city ghetto; if you placed enough poor people together you were guaranteed certain things. You were guaranteed that there would be more poverty and drug use, lower self-esteem, an increase in teen pregnancies and the dropout rate, and higher taxes. There was also something else you were guaranteed: more dependent, liberal voters.

I was astounded by my theory. As a young liberal I even doubted its truth. But in my research I could not find one poor neighborhood that had ever voted conservative. The poorer a community was, the stronger its vote for liberals. So if you were a liberal politician, why would you want prosperity to come these communities? If you were a liberal and understood that the more prosperous a community was the more likely they would be to vote you out of office, *what would you do*?

Liberals are not stupid. Like every politician, they want to gain and retain power. And liberals know their power comes from delivering benefits to the poor, not from setting poor people free.

Those mean-spirited conservatives that I hated also understood how to play the political and social games. They knew the more prosperous a community became, the more likely they would be to vote for a conservative candidate. That is why conservatives believe in family control of children, support local control of education, and promote tax relief for freedom-seeking working people.

Conservatives understood that their support came from voters and consumers who are freedom-seeking people. You cannot be free and dependent at the same time. You must be either free or dependent. In a way, I confirmed my professors' statement. Liberals *were* for the poor, and conservatives *were* for the rich. Liberals wanted there to be as many poor people as possible; however, conservatives did not want *anyone* to be poor.

Chapter 4

Freedom is Risky for Master

Master always tells you that freedom is bad and only a fool would seek it

Master tells his slaves that all they desire comes from him. If there is a crisis, only he can solve it. If you need more food, he is the source. Your food does not come from your own hard work; your food comes from a bowl, and master owns the bowl. If you have a crime problem, he has a crime bill. If your children cannot read or write, you must turn to him to better educate them for you. You must depend upon him to take the necessary action to solve all of your problems.

You cannot think of one problem facing us today that does not require a government solution. Big or small, all must have government input before the problem can be resolved. This reminds me of a parent with a small, defenseless child. Everything the child wants or needs requires action from the parent. If the child is hungry, sleepy or thirsty, the parent must act before the child can be satisfied. Everything in the child's life depends upon the parent's permission or action. So it is with our "nanny-state" government. If you do not think you are a slave or dependent upon master, then think of yourself as being a child as far as the government is concerned.

Everything from raising your children to job security and retirement depends upon the government. Just as with a parent, you do it for the child's own good and safety. Without our government, we would die without seat belts. Without government, we would pump gas with cigarettes in our mouths. There is nothing our government will not do for us, because we are not safe without them.

This is the same message the old slave master gave his slaves. *You cannot survive without me. Your existence depends upon me taking care of you. I am nice and benevolent and will provide for you even as you get old and sick. You are not independent; you are dependent.*

If you need something, go to your misleaders and they will come to me. Do not ever try to gain freedom on your own—that is dangerous. I will tax you, regulate you, or imprison you if you try to gain too much freedom from me.

Master takes 15% of your income, and promises to give it back to you when you retire

An example of how this modern form of slavery works is the deferred-return Social Security program. Most workers have a portion of their salary confiscated by the government to pay for what they think is a "retirement program." The government taxes you when they take your money, and then places it in their bank to collect interest during your entire working career. Then after you retire, they will tax you *again* when you collect it. But they will not give it back to you at all if you do not please them. If you were too independent-minded as a worker and created alternative income, you will not get your retirement money that has been confiscated by the government. If you make too much money during your retirement from your investments, the government will say that you do not need the Social Security money they took from you, and they will give your money to people who have remained on their plantation of poverty.

So, your money has been taken away from you for 20 or 30 years, collecting interest in the government vault, and you get little or nothing back. Those who foolishly depended upon the government to take care of them will find themselves in a predicament. They will be dependent upon master for the pennies in their pension and will have to go begging for prescription drugs and other health benefits when they need them the most. They will still pay taxes on their home and income, and their children will pay taxes on anything they leave to them when they die.

What is so amazing about the system is how master has gotten us to fight against the reformers in order to keep it in place. I know a man who makes $3 million a month in residual income. That means his income is not dependent upon him doing anything. He is past retirement age but still pays $15,000 per month in Social Security taxes. His money is confiscated under false pretenses because no one expects him to ever get this back as retirement income. The percentage of income taken from workers has no set dollar limit. However, the amount of income you get back *does* have a limit.

Liberals understand that you would become financially independent if you were able to save that 15% of hard-earned money that was confiscated from you. By simply placing it in government savings bonds, a 401(k) program, or a passbook savings account, you would retire wealthy.

Within one generation we would not need vouchers because grandmother could take care of the private school. We would not need Aid to Women with Dependent Children programs because grandfather could take care of them. Within one generation we would not need liberals…and *that* is why we do not have a real retirement program.

They want you to pay taxes on your home every year and then pay capital gains taxes when you sell it. They want you to spend 30 years paying property taxes in addition to the sales tax on everything you ever purchased to improve and maintain your home, and then force your children to pay an inheritance tax when you leave it to them. This will keep your children dependent upon master instead of honoring the sacrifices made by previous generations.

Chapter 5

Everyone Deserves Freedom

I was a militant but it dawned on me that I was making more slaves. I began to understand what I was fighting for. It was for freedom. And not just freedom for black people because it was not a black and white issue. I was fighting for *freedom*. No one could be free until *all* of us were free. We were all slaves—black *and* white. Since we had been taught to hate and distrust one another, we were actually fighting to keep master in control while thinking we were better than the "other" slaves on the opposite side of the fence.

White Americans are just as stuck in the plantation mentality as black or brown Americans. Multiculturalism divides us over our differences and has us fighting for our own perceived piece of the pie. Instead of fighting

43

against master's education system—which only turns out more and more obedient slaves—we fight each other over master's grant programs.

This plantation mentality is not about skin color, income level, or education. It is motivated and controlled by the desire of one people to have power over another. It can only be thought of in these terms. If you think you are going to counter master's plantation mentality by convincing master to grant you your freedom, you are wasting your time.

Master has never given up his slaves; they have always had to struggle for their freedom. When pressured enough, master will pretend he is granting freedom. He will simply change the name from "slavery" to "sharecropping" and keep you in the fields.

Chapter 6

What You do with the Rope Tells the Story

You have to understand the power master has over his slaves. They do not resist; they agree with master. The slave believes his position is natural and only hopes master will take good care of him. He will not even fight to have a new master because he *knows* his old master. Even if his master is cruel, he does not want a new one. Therefore, the slave will vote to support his master's programs.

All master has to do is tell his slaves that any changes to his programs that are already in place will keep him (master) from being able to take care of his slaves, so the slaves will fight to keep master in power.

The slave mentality has the slave sincerely

believing that his condition is hopeless. Master controls every aspect of the slave's life—even his own self-perception. Master controls the news, culture, and education that the slave receives. Master will also define the slave's nature, motivation, and goals for him. The slave will always strive to please master, so he keeps a suspicious and watchful eye on any other slave that is trying to escape the plantation.

Master does not need to keep watch over his slaves; the slaves will do this for him. They allow their children to be mis-educated and themselves to be overtaxed. If you try to help slaves, you are in for a real workout. The slave will fight you more than master will!

If you try to encourage and help a slave abandon his plantation mentality, you may be surprised to see most of the resistance coming from the slave himself. But when people are able to pull themselves out of the plantation mentality—and there have been many—the pathway to freedom will become clearer to them.

You may be one of these overcomers on the path to freedom. You see the way out of poverty, dependency, and *master's* control and will follow that pathway to freedom. And like all decent people, when you find the way to freedom, safety, or privilege, you always want to go and tell your friends and relatives. This is where the problem begins. Telling slaves about freedom can be very frustrating.

Why is it clear to you, but so difficult—even frustrating—when you try to tell others? Why is it possible for you to see a great business opportunity so clearly, but your wife, mother, son or best friend cannot see any of the possibilities?

The answer is easy: you were thinking like a prisoner looking for a way out and your friends are still thinking like slaves with no way out. The slave believes that the very notion of freedom is bad. Master has convinced him that if he were set free he would starve to death. The slave believes master is taking care of him out of the goodness of his heart so he tries to please him.

The slave believes your efforts to seek economic freedom are an insult to him and to master. You are ungrateful for the leadership of the plantation and master's efforts to take care of you. That is why your slave friends and relatives cannot see your great business opportunity. You cannot make the slave understand, so you must leave him in his current state of mind and move on with your business. The slave will only poison your plans with negative thinking. *You may want to throw a rope over the fence for your slave relatives to join you, but it will be of no use. You may insist on giving a rope of freedom to all of your friends, but it will not work.*

While you are using the rope to help you get over the fence, the slave sees the rope as a lynching tool. The slave resists the offer of your rope and thinks your help will harm him—and harm you. The slave may get very defensive over your rope and wonder why you are trying to get him in trouble with master. He's wondering, *"Why are you trying to lynch your friend?"*

But if you throw a rope to another freedom-loving prisoner like yourself, they will thank you. You do not have to tell a prisoner he is in prison. He understands that once he is outside those gates, he will have freedom. A prisoner will spend twenty years looking for a way to escape. He will try many things; most will fail. But his failures will not deter him because his desire for freedom is what motivates him. When another prisoner sees your rope, he will immediately recognize it as what he has been looking for. He will grab the rope and pull himself to freedom.

If you throw a rope to a prisoner, he will thank and praise you. He will call you his friend as he takes hold of the rope and climbs out of the prison. This is why we need to seek out other prisoners *first* and work on the slaves later.

Some prisoners have been so beaten up trying to escape that they may not have a lot of strength left. They still have the desire, but no strength. Your rope is a means of escape, but they may have to tie knots in the rope. A knot will provide something to grab hold of. It will give the prisoner a place to rest his feet during the difficult climb out. You must help the other prisoners tie the knots in those ropes.

Every business meeting a prisoner attends is a knot in their rope, and everyone that they show the plan of escape to is another knot in their rope. Prisoners tie knots in their rope every time they share information about freedom with other prisoners. The more knots, the easier the climb.

However, if you bring *slaves* into your business while trying to tie knots in your rope—watch out. Fellow prisoners will tie knots; slaves will *oil* your rope. Slaves do not want you or anybody else to escape master's plantation. They are usually slave managers and fear master's punishment for your escape.

They will pour oil on your rope in the form of negative comments and attitudes. They will constantly tell others that your plan will only benefit you—not them. They will look for every opportunity to dissuade your fellow prisoners from following you to freedom. Keep the slaves away from the escape committee and watch out for the oil. Use the oil to light your lamp on the pathway to freedom, not to oil your rope.

Chapter 7

The Test—
Are You a Slave or a Prisoner?

Is your rope greased or dry?
If you cannot wait for the morning commute
  to start...
If you can't wait to see your boss...
If you're wondering when you'll get that
  promotion you earned last year...
If you find people either boring or scary when
  they speak about their own business...then
  YOU ARE A SLAVE!

YOU ARE A PRISONER IF:
  You have found your rope and are excited.
  You have never allowed failure to stop you from
    trying.
  You have never been content satisfying master.
  You look at successful people and wonder,
    "When *will* I?" instead of "Why *can't* I?"

The enemy's most powerful weapon is to convince you that you're a slave. So, as you build your business, remember these four things. Place them on your office wall or your refrigerator.

1. Success really *is* available to you.
2. You *can* be free.
3. Don't let *anyone* grease your rope.
4. Never, *never, NEVER* give up.

Whether you are a prisoner or a slave should be easy to figure out. How are you handling the rope? Are you tying knots, or oiling the rope? Do you think you can, or are you afraid to try? Are you so comfortable on the plantation that the sight of a rope scares you? The truth will set you free.

Accepting the truth will compel you to take action—which is precisely why so many people are determined to resist the truth. They know you are logical and are making sense. But they also know that if they accept the notion of self-reliance and independence, they must *do* something. A lot of people are lazy and the truth is too much of a burden, so they downplay it. They spend time countering the truth with weak arguments, or try to change the subject just enough so that you will get off the topic. If someone doesn't want to take action, they will reject the truth.

Some abused wives reject the truth because they don't want to leave an abusive husband. They have doubts about who will take care of their kids. If you *tell* them to leave, they won't understand. But once *they* realize their need to change, you won't have to tell them to leave any more.

Once you accept the truth and begin to move towards freedom, there will be some other changes in your life. New friendships are an inevitable change that comes with success.

Chapter 8

The New Underground Railroad

People who refuse to live in a nation of slavery are my heroes

History gives us the opportunity to learn about slavery and the pathway to freedom. We can examine the nations of the world and see the escape routes of people who were held in bondage. Seldom did the slaves successfully rise up against their masters—at least not without substantial help from people outside the slave community. The Hebrews had a long history of rising up against their masters, usually by following a spiritual leader within the community. But most slave communities relied upon the sacrificial help of others.

The slaves of America tried many times to rebel against their masters. There were over

250 slave revolts and rebellions recorded in American history. Only the people of Haiti successfully overthrew their master. But Haiti needed the combined help of England, Spain and France to do so. The slaves of America could not have obtained their freedom without the help of others.

Master held all of the cards. He controlled the news, the self-perception, and the motivation of the slaves. Master told the slaves that freedom was negative and dangerous. The very thought of freedom was a frightful thing to slaves. *Who would feed them? How would they get shelter?* They only understood that master was the source of everything they had. Good or bad, they needed master—or so he said.

Slaves were told that anyone who left the plantation would never come back because they would die in the woods. Without master there were no means of survival. Slaves were told the freedom fighters hated them because they wanted to take them away from master's care. After all, master always had food for them, took care of them when they were sick, and gave them a roof over their heads.

Today, master is still scaring the slaves and telling them to watch out for the freedom fighters. The slaves are told that the freedom fighters actually want them to fend for themselves. Master, on the other hand, has given them food and low-income housing and will always have jobs for them. Master has educated the parents and will do the same for their children...if they will just serve him.

Master has told the freedom fighters that the slaves love slavery. After all, they are always singing, dancing, and acting happy. Master said they were content because they were secure, and he would take care of them as long as they did his will. Today, master is saying that the new slaves are content because he takes good care of them. Master allows them to vote for his selected representatives, gives them some semblance of schooling, and keeps enough drugs (legal and illegal) available to dull most of their pain.

In the past, the lies of the old masters could only last for so long. Soon, escaped slaves began to make their way north and news of the horrors of slavery became known. But this did not help those still on the plantation. It did not give hope to those still getting all of their news from master. Someone had to go back and tell them the truth about freedom. This is what we really need today.

Safe houses sent escaped slaves back to the plantation to free the rest of the slaves

Why did escaped slaves have to go back to their own plantation with the word of freedom? The abolitionists couldn't go because they were too conspicuous and it would not benefit anyone. However, they were willing to put their fortunes, management abilities, and experience to the task of ending slavery; but escaped slaves themselves had to go back to the plantations and risk their own lives for their fellow slaves. They were the only ones who could accomplish the task.

The escaped slaves—who had longed for freedom so much that they risked death and the unknown—ventured back into the South for one thing stronger than their desire for freedom: love and hate. Love for their loved ones left behind, and hatred for a system. The escaped slave, even after reaching the higher goal of freedom, still returned for others. They believed that no one was free unless *all* were free.

It was important for escaped slaves to return to their own plantations. Master had warned all the slaves that escaping the safety of his plantation meant certain death. They were told of starvation, wild animals, bounty hunters, and other horrors that awaited them on the way.

I have seen freedom—lets go!

The escaped slaves returned to their own plantations to prove master was a liar. When slaves received a knock on their door late at night, they saw a friend or relative standing there: not a stranger, but someone they knew and remembered—and who master had told them was dead. Master could not tell the slaves to watch out for members of the Underground Railroad. He could not make them believe it was a trick because the slaves *knew* their rescuers.

The success of the Underground Railroad was due to the willingness of the escaped slaves to return to their plantations. They told the slaves that master was lying to them about freedom. They had seen freedom and freedom was real—they had been there—and promised that they would show them the way. They told the slaves that master did not want them to understand that freedom was attainable. The freedom fighters assured the slaves that they would be led to freedom. They knew the path and would take them along the way. They promised the slaves that if they got lost, they would find them; if they stumbled, they would pick them up. They told the slaves that there were many people willing to help them and show them to the next stop along the way.

Freedom had come to the plantation, but only for those who were willing to leave. The Underground Railroad was not meant for slaves who worried about master, overseers, or slave drivers. It was not a place for debate or concerns over master's feelings. If the slaves feared master, they stayed; if they doubted the freedom fighter, they stayed. The Underground Railroad to freedom was only available to those who were willing to come aboard.

A new generation of safe houses is beginning to emerge in living rooms across America

Today, the wage slaves are still told that freedom is negative and unattainable. Master is still telling his slaves that the very goal of freedom is dangerous for them. The wage slaves of today still cannot find freedom on their own and need the help of the same old-time freedom fighters of yesteryear. They cannot escape master's plantation without freedom fighters helping them.

Those who have found their way to freedom must continue to go back and tell others. They must be willing to show the way for all who are willing to go. They must travel back to the plantation they escaped from to tell their relatives and friends about freedom. They must be the ones to counter the lies and deception fostered by master. Only the escaped slaves can reach the minds and souls of the wage slaves. Their personal testimonies are the only words of encouragement that can reach the slaves.

Today, we need to encourage this NEW UNDERGROUND RAILROAD. We need safe houses all over America that will tell the truth about real freedom—ECONOMIC FREEDOM. The New Underground Railroad is sending escaped slaves back to their own plantations so they can spread the word of real freedom.

Economic freedom is the key to real freedom because it gives *you* control over your life and the lives of your family members. It allows you to make your own decisions regarding education, retirement, and even medical care. All of the controls master now enjoys would evaporate if the slaves had economic freedom. The New Underground Railroad will concentrate on bringing information to the slaves about the pathway to freedom. It will counter the negative thinking of the slave mentality.

Like their namesakes of old, these new freedom fighters are going back to tell the slaves that master was lying to them about the dangers of freedom and the benefits of opportunity. Master may be able to control the news, culture and education, but he cannot control the New Underground Railroad.

It is getting harder to tell the wage slaves that they cannot make it without master when their sons and daughters are coming back with news of freedom. It is getting frustrating for master to train up new slaves to serve his own children when the children of slaves are bringing back reports about freedom.

Freedom has been transformed from just a dream into an attainable goal, and the goal now has a plan to go with it. Many wage slaves are working their plan and master is feeling the effect. Freedom is available to everyone regardless of race, gender, age, nationality, physical challenges, place of residence, etc. The power to succeed is within your grasp. In fact, it is now possible to do business all over the world from your own living room.

Chapter 9

Understand how to be Financially Independent

Have you heard of people who have made and lost many fortunes? How did they make fortunes more than once? How can someone make and lose millions of dollars and have the skills to make it again? We can either look at the mistakes that caused them to lose their money or understand that they must know how to *make* money. In order to recover from losing a fortune you must have the confidence that you can re-establish the wealth you once had.

I know many people who have had tremendous financial success, and I have divided them into two groups. One group has made their money by creating a business or service that has become successful. They were able to develop an infrastructure with bankers, suppliers and customers to create a high level of income.

The second group of successful people created a *technique* to success. They followed a structure developed on business principles that could be used as a model for many business applications. Therefore, the people in this group can make and lose a fortune over and over again. They will never be broke because they understand how money flows through them.

I know a man who is one of the business owners in a multi-level organization. He has worked in this business for many years and is enjoying the fruits of that success. But his success is not based upon the ability to move his merchandise: it is based upon his ability to move people. To motivate another person toward success is the key to his and others' success. Since he uses this well-established formula, no one can keep this man poor.

He understands how to motivate others toward success, and their success ensures his. You could take my friend away from his business, and take away all of his money—along with all of his contacts—and it will not matter. He will still make money again because he understands the pathway to freedom. That is what the slave needs:

someone with the knowledge and willingness to share the pathway.

While my first group of wealthy friends will share their time and friendship, they will not share the secrets of their success with me. I cannot ask my friends who own a major national beer company to show me how to brew and distribute beer. Why would they help me to compete against them and their children? But the gentleman with the multi-level business is eager to help me duplicate his success because it will benefit him. In fact, it would benefit him even if I were to grow my business bigger than his.

More importantly, this man is motivated by the desire to help others get to freedom. He is not motivated by money or power. His success is greater than he has ever hoped for, but he is still driving home the message of freedom to all who will listen. You, too, should be motivated by freedom, not merely by money.

That is how the New Underground Railroad works, and as it grows it will be made up of leaders with the knowledge and dedication to lead wage slaves to economic freedom. The foundations of slavery are not rooted in race, color, nationality, or gender. Slavery is based upon power and weakness, and is perpetuated by dependency and co-dependency.

Chapter 10

Know No Boundaries

We have leaders and we have misleaders. *Which ones motivate you?* Misleaders know that if they keep us focused on our differences, we won't concentrate on what they are doing. No one will knowingly follow a misleader; he must trick you into thinking you are being led. You must develop enough knowledge to recognize the subtle differences between following and being led.

Anyone under the influence of a misleader will accept his anti-success approach and will voluntarily keep themselves and all others down. They will not do the things necessary for success, and will not want you to, either.

The misleaders claim victim status for us and convince us of how terribly we have been treated by other groups. But master will never remind us how much better off we all are as Americans than where we came from. You cannot find black people, white people, poor people, or any other people who are better off anywhere else than in America.

You can complain about your special group's problems all day long, but you will not be able to find any country where that group is better off than in America. The reason is clear. We, as Americans, have taken cultures from around the world and blended them into one, unique culture.

We have a culture that is the envy of the entire world. We have combined all of these cultures into one culture—the American culture—and that is who we are. If you were born here or have joined us here, you belong here. However, you are not an African-American, Native-American, or European-American—you are something far greater…an <u>American</u>.

Master wants you to give him the credit for all of the developments in American culture, history, and science. He also encourages you to participate in something called "multiculturalism"—separate but equal subcultures—which is a sham.

Many misleaders use multiculturalism for

their own benefit. They divide and conquer. But who benefits the most from multiculturalism? Ask yourself this question: Who will lose their position of power and authority when multiculturalism is exposed for the lie it is? There will be a long line of self-appointed misleaders with no followers. They will no longer have large groups to represent when they lobby master for more benefits, subsidies, welfare and housing, etc. It will be up to self-sufficient, independent-minded individuals to support themselves and their families in an American culture of equality.

There are no real limits or boundaries to your success, just hesitation brought on by the plantation mentality. You are only limited by the restrictions you have placed on yourself. The misleaders want you to believe that your goals are unattainable on your own so that you will need *them* to succeed. But what is the misleaders idea of "success"? It's for you to be provided with master's substandard level of housing, food, education, and health care. If liberal politicians continue to give you goodies and handouts, they know you will keep them in power by voting for them.

However, master does not want you to experience any level of true success at all because he doesn't want you to compete against him and his children. He wants you to build the bricks for his child's kingdom, not for your own child. Master will try to convince you that your only hope and pleasure can come as a result of pleasing him.

Do not let master set your boundaries. Do not even set them for yourself. You should have no boundaries!

Chapter 11

The Courage to be Free

DARE TO BE RICH! It is a dare because many of us are terrified at the prospect of financial success. We look at life as if there are only two types of people: successful and struggling to be successful. We become critical if one of our friends tries to change the position in life we have assigned to him.

We become frightened of the things we know will lead to success. The reason there is a fear of success is the same reason the slaves were always afraid of freedom...master.

When the children of Israel were taken into slavery they stayed in Egypt over 400 years. But after gaining their freedom they began to complain that Moses was not taking care of them. Many had not wanted to leave in the first place, and held memories of a secure life on Pharaoh's plantation.

The newly-freed slaves longed to return to slavery because of the feeding and care Pharaoh provided for them. They forgot about the murder, hard labor, and mistreatment. They did not remember why their fathers had prayed to be set free. They only remembered the security of master's plantation.

Once you have been frightened, all you want is safety—not freedom. If master can convince you that there is a crisis, he knows you will look to him to protect you. He protects you by taking away your freedom and then controlling you...for your own good, of course.

As long as you are not responsible for yourself, master will be. From seat belt laws to gun control, all is motivated by fear. We allow unconstitutional laws and regulations to be passed because we are afraid of the dark.

Years ago, 70,000 jobs were lost in the Pacific Northwest due to fears over the safety of a sub-species of spotted owl that, in fact, was never in any danger. Families were destroyed and businesses were forced to shut down—all out of fear.

The Solution—
a) Take away the fear of being free

The only way for the slave to find freedom is to confront and overcome his fears. If he is paralyzed with fear he will never walk towards freedom. The slave who believes he cannot make the journey will not even start it. We must understand the mental state slavery breeds and that it is mostly a mirage.

Master and his slave managers are very good at instilling and controlling fear in their slaves. If we could overcome our fear of freedom, we would be free. But how do we do it?

b) Find a safe house

How can a slave bring himself to think as a free person? Well, how has it been done before? If we look at the slaves of America, Africa or Israel, we find that their freedom was won through the help of outsiders. Freedom must come from freedom-loving people.

In America, freedom will come through the efforts of those who have escaped and are now enjoying the benefits and blessings of freedom, and through those people who celebrate a rich tradition of freedom.

Freedom-loving Americans refused to live in a country that allowed men to be enslaved. They joined hands with freedom-loving slaves who were determined to escape the plantation. Both groups loved freedom so much that they risked all they had for freedom. It is important to understand that the old Underground Railroad was operated by free people. Both blacks and whites were free people risking everything for others' freedom, not their own.

The Northerners were rich and independent, and the escaped slaves were already in the North and were free. They organized the old Underground Railroad for others, not for themselves. NO ONE IS FREE UNTIL **ALL** ARE FREE!

That is the same spirit we need today: escaped slaves returning to the plantation to spread the word of freedom; abolitionist funding and organization for the great escape; and both fighting for the true American spirit—that of freedom.

Chapter 12

Choose Freedom Over Slavery

When I was a young college student I was so full of hate and fear that I could not think straight. While attending U.C. Berkeley I became so full of hatred towards America that I could not take care of my family or be successful. I eventually learned *why* I hated and what it was doing to me. It became clear that all of my hatred was being fueled by a defeatist, victimized view of myself. How could I be angry with others if I was in charge of myself? If I was not in charge of myself, why direct my anger at others? It was very clear: if you are in charge, you cannot be angry. I decided to give up the anger.

When I gave up that barrier I realized that the only force on the planet strong enough to hold Mason Weaver down was Mason Weaver. I was fighting against myself like a puppy chasing his own tail. The harder you fight, the worse you feel about yourself.

What will it be—knots or oil?

Who's going to tie the knots in your rope? Who's going to control your rope? Who's going to support you in the effort needed to bring you up from slavery to freedom? We all need help—but not from someone who will help themselves *to* us. You must travel the road to success yourself. But who will lead you to that road? Who will provide security for you while you are traveling the road to freedom...economic freedom?

Think about your condition in life. If you want to know where you are going and how you will end up, look at others around you. Have you seen the old man taking tickets at the movie theater? He is standing beside a 16-year-old because he has to work *after* his retirement. Trust me, he did not start off 25 years ago with the goal of ending up working back at that theater. In fact, he probably started there at age 16, left home to go to college, graduated and got a great job on the plantation. He believed master when master promised to take a large portion of his income and make him "socially secure" after his retirement. He felt comfortable allowing master to manage his healthcare plan and every other aspect of his life.

But now he has retired and found out that he cannot depend upon master. He must return to his first job in a fast food restaurant, movie theater or parking garage, and he *still* must pay a portion of the cotton he picks to master. He still depends upon master to take care of his children. He still expects master to educate his grandchildren and provide money for his elderly care. He is also still afraid of success.

He will tell you why you can't compete with others. He will tell you why you cannot—and should not—compete against master and master's children. He will remind you of the days when he tried to obtain his freedom, and also of the day he stopped trying. He cannot allow you to think about freedom, because he is afraid of being proven wrong.

He will remind you of the personal problems that stand in your way: your mother drank too much, your father abandoned you, and your income is just not high enough. You cannot compete, so do not try. He wants you to think like a slave because all *he* has left is his master.

Just take a glimpse into the future. *Is he you?* If you are not in control, master is in control. If you believe master's lies about your life, then you have no life. If you believe master, then you and your children will serve him. But if you believe in yourself, then master has no more power over you.

Three words that will make you free– Independent Business Owner

Master knows there are three words you must never understand, and his greatest fear is for you to comprehend the reality and accessibility of these three words. He has formulated an entire education system that is designed to keep the knowledge of these three little words away from you.

Independent: *Empowered, in charge, and uncompromising*. This person could be trapped on a plantation but will never surrender his mind. He will fail in attempt after attempt to

78

escape but will continue to press on in his search for independence. Because of his mental state, he will never be a slave. We have the option to choose one of two destinies—slavery or freedom.

Business: *An economic system that is centered on the revenue stream.* There is a reason they call it currency: it flows. You only need to find a way into the revenue stream and cash will come in all around you. The best way to enter the revenue stream and generate cash flow is with your own business. Once established, it can secure your economic freedom for generations to come. Not only will it provide security for you and allow you to take immediate control over your life, it will provide you with the power to influence the lifestyle of generations of your descendants.

Owner: *Master knows you cannot have two masters on one plantation.* Get your own plantation! You must be the one responsible and in total control of this plantation. If you have to pick cotton, make sure it is your own cotton.

Independent Business Owners: *This attitude will change your way of thinking.* If you are thinking like a business owner and begin to act like one, you will begin to act like a free person.

Conclusion

Take control yourself! If you want to be in control of your life, understand that no one will give it to you. If you desire to provide for your own future, it must be based upon your own action—not the actions of others. Your success in life should not be dependent upon the approval, action, or authority of another person or a government program.

If you're tired of not having control, then change your course. Begin taking responsibility for your life by acting on the knowledge that you are free. If you are free, not only does master no longer have any control over you, he has no responsibility *for* you. If you are hungry, you must feed yourself. If you need housing, you must provide it for yourself. You cannot be free from master and still look to him for anything.

It may not be fair that you worked so hard on master's plantation and now he won't give you a safe, comfortable way to escape. I know you farmed his land, milked his cows, and paid large portions of your income to him in taxes. Too bad.

81

If you are going to leave, leave and do not turn back. If you wait for master to give you what you deserve, you will continue to stay on the plantation.

Master is not concerned with your anger and frustration. It does not bother him that you are demanding part of his plantation. He wants you to protest, demonstrate, and rebel at the injustices he presides over so that you will be fooled into believing you're making progress. You can stir up all the trouble you want…just as long as you do not *act* on your power to change your life.

Master will tolerate your anger as long as you continue to depend upon him for your freedom. Do not wait for what he can give you. You can achieve everything he has if you compete directly against him.

My dad says that only a fool will starve in the land of plenty. Well, we have plenty of opportunity to be free and succeed to whatever level we dare to. Don't be successful to spite master. Do it for yourself because you have the freedom to do so.

Freedom is good. Take control of your life. You can do it!

God bless you.

82